The Weight of Two Oranges

The Weight of Two Oranges

Words and Images
by Lynda Wilde

Wintergreen Studios Press
Township of South Frontenac
PO Box 75, Yarker, ON, Canada K0K 3N0

Copyright © 2024, with copyright retained by the author. All rights reserved under the International and Pan-American Copyright Conventions. No part of this book may be reproduced in any form or by electronic or mechanical means, including information storage and retrieval systems, without permission in writing from the publisher, except by a reviewer, who may quote brief passages in a review. The views expressed in this work are those of the author and do not necessarily reflect those of the publisher. Wintergreen Studios Press (WSP) gratefully acknowledges financial support from Wintergreen Studios.

Words and images by Lynda Wilde
Book design by Rena Upitis
Cover photo by Lynda Wilde

Composed in Calibri and Raceway; typefaces designed by Lucas de Groot and Zavier Cabarga, respectively.

Library and Archives Canada Cataloguing in Publication
Wilde, Lynda.
The Weight of Two Oranges/Lynda Wilde
ISBN: 978-1-989321-26-3
Poetry — General.
I. Title. The Weight of Two Oranges.
Legal Deposit — Library and Archives Canada

The rich imagery of Lynda Wilde's language combines with her spare, stunning illustrations into a poetry of contrasts: the familiar with the exotic, ice with colour, quiet pleasures with vivid memories and dreams. This is a story of love and loss; a portrait of the places of her heart — of all our hearts.

~ Susan Haldane, *Hard Bargain Road*

Lynda Wilde's writing is achingly beautiful. She draws readers into each scene with exquisite imagery, adding color, flavor, and precise language to each piece.

~ Arvilla Fee, Managing Editor San Antonio Review

Across years and across landscapes, from Mexico to Eastern Ontario Lynda Wilde addresses issues of belonging, loss, climate change and love—the large in the small, all that makes daily life matter.

~ Susan Wismer, *Hag Dances*

With a strong eye for design and composition, Lynda Wilde has developed a compelling personal photographic style.

~ Richard Martin, acclaimed Canadian photographer, long-time contributor to *Photo Life* magazine

Contents

Season of Jacarandas 1

I thought I saw us today 2

El Danzon 3

Why Broccoli? 5

The Weight of Two Oranges 7

Oriole 8

Taking the Measure 9

The Irredeemables 10

Flight 11

Visitation 12

Redwings 13

The Weight of It 14

Birds During a Pandemic 16

Through the Glass 17

Saturday Afternoon Confession 19

Los Más Bonitos 20

Los Antepasados 21

Samana Santa 23

Evening Shades 24

The Bend in the Road 26

Swimming Lesson 27

Casa Divina 28

Gallina 30

Like a Blue Sterile Cloth 31

Pata de Elefante 33

Someone Would Find It … 34

All the Summer Birds Have Left 35

What to Dream of Then 36

Ask Me Now 37

On the last day of the world 38

Painkiller 40

Tell all the truth but tell it slant —
Emily Dickinson

Season of Jacarandas

it inserts itself quietly into her psyche
it will not go unnoticed
that month of March
a vague stirring in the back of the mind
dust to be shaken from shoes

it lets her sleepwalk for a while
warm breeze across the shoulders
before suggesting she has been
too long with the habit of contentment
too easy among the jacarandas

I thought I saw us today

in a Mexican town
at a table in a courtyard
a quiet *barrio*

late lunch, margaritas
under jacarandas
we had grown old

as we thought we would
that day in trendy
Toronto, a quiet space

beneath black branches
white wine, yellow leaves
heavy with autumn

falling around us

El Danzon

I am in the *zocalo* tonight. On Wednesday nights a marimba band assembles and old folks gather to dance. They dress in finery and move sedately with carefully choreographed steps. An audience watches. I am seated on a stone wall observing intently when I feel a tap on my shoulder. It is an elderly man. Will I dance with him? *No thank you.*
I am in casual clothes and shy of lights, an audience, unfamiliar dance steps.
He persists. *I'm sorry.* I try to explain, *I can't.*
Why not? He is puzzled. *Is there something wrong with your heart?*
I leave soon after and walk home wondering if there is something wrong with my heart. It's December 20th, the shortest day of the year. I could have spent part of it dancing.

Why Broccoli?

He steps off the curb, avoids being struck by drivers running the red light. Mexican drivers make their own rules and respect them among themselves. The young man understands this and now stands before a jumble of vehicles, four rows *mas o menos*. Ragged and unwashed, he holds five worn tennis balls. He knows he is good with three but perhaps five will impress, bring in some much needed cash. He has been practicing at night in an alleyway with other hustlers and now launches the five balls into the bright blue over his head. I am in my old Rav4 and high enough to get a good view from the edge of the pack of cars. I wince as he misses a ball and runs chasing all five between cars. I catch myself holding my breath as he starts a second time. My stomach tightens as he fumbles a third time, a fourth. Street performers must time their act exactly to the light. His time is running out. Drivers are revving engines. Am I the only one still silently cheering him on? He drops the balls a fifth time and the light turns green. Pushed on in traffic I catch a glimpse of him in my side mirror, hand extended as cars pass by, no one offering a peso.

Why not do something you're good at, I wonder, pick a money-maker?

Early in my visits to Mexico I spent a dreary winter trying to learn Spanish in a small town where it rained most days. A tired sun struggled out between clouds in late afternoon and worn wooden tables were dragged out into the square. People gathered for *cervezas and antojitos* and day after dismal day an old woman appeared, went from table to table offering a limp head of broccoli. Never a sale.

The Weight of Two Oranges

it was not constant concern
for the troubled planet
harnessing her thoughts
that day so much as the weight
of two oranges in a cloth bag
slung over her shoulder
the careful keeping to the
shade side of the street
vines flowering sun-stained adobe
cobbles slanting toward home
where stone steps leading
to the street below marked
the edge of the hot day—
it was the market woman
fingering brown spotted eggs
praising her beautiful hens
eyes above mask smiling up at the
gringa willing to pay five pesos
an egg all nine in the basket sold
a day's work complete
and the *gringa* left content
with a world spiralling more easily
now around a few eggs
and the weight of two oranges

Oriole

I returned early this year
pushed north by a pandemic
to wait while you
moved up the continent
at your own pace.
Impatient, I placed orange halves
among the lilacs to lure you
to my garden.

I sip spring wine and watch
through thin May days
while the sun angles north
and the ghost of my neighbour
comes down the path
to admire your orange flash
and, forgetting that she is dead,
asks why I am waiting alone.

Taking the Measure

A woman is crossing a parking lot to her car, her arms around a brown bag holding bottles of wine. As she approaches she looks up to see a man standing between her car and a brick wall as if waiting for her. *Could you give me some money?* He is stocky, wears jeans and a faded windbreaker, one knee bent up so that the sole of his boot rests against the wall. His hands move around in his pockets. She avoids his glance, looks down into the bag and then off to the side where two crows are standing on the roof of a car, getting ready to outwit a seagull. The woman has only a credit card in the pocket of her own jeans. She looks back at the man, takes the measure of him. The seagull is nearing a hunk of bread on the pavement. One crow flies to his side and distracts him. The other swoops down, grabs the bread, and the pair fly away together.
The woman opens her car and finds a bill. *Thanks* the stranger says and now she looks at him more directly.
What are you going to do with it?
Buy a drink.
Good, she thinks. *You look like you need a stiff one.*
The seagull is bewildered, walks round in circles.

The Irredeemables

She opened the inside wooden door. An old man stood on the other side of the glass. He was tall and thin with rimless glasses, heavy woollen overcoat and cap. He opened his mouth as if to speak but then just pushed a pamphlet up against the pane. She recognized his gesture as an attempt to save her and waved a hand 'no, too late, too late'. He dropped his arm and, pamphlet in hand, slouched back down the porch steps. It was a cold April morning, sun struggling to break grey cloud. She closed the door, went back to her chair beside the fire, savoured her damnation. She couldn't help but think of him, the old proselytizer, adding her to his list of irredeemables. She could have stretched her stingy spirit, let him at least try. How many rejections needed, she wondered, for him to win his badge of merit. Perhaps he was the one feeling sorry for her, forsaken as the lilac tapping at the window, grey, spindly, bud and leaf as distant as Mexico. She thought she was finished with Mexico, its dust, its heat, its big unashamed blue sky. Just now she missed its ease.

Flight

Pushed from a sanctuary high up, you landed
hard, mess of soft plumage, spindly legs
long, unstable on the sidewalk.
You stood and uttered a pathetic cry,
tried to walk — no instinct for flight.
I wished to nest you again, offer you
a second more confident start.
Cement is an unforgiving surface for a fledgling
filled with fear, siblings scattered, mother flown.
Lift your beady eyes aloft, sense your sisters
in full flight. Let your little bird brain take it in.
Then shelter in grass by the picket fence
stay safe one long and lonely night.
Strength will secure your tiny heart, penetrate
your pulse. You will feel it in your feathers.

Visitation

she thought if she ever saw him again he would be wearing a tux

she'd raise her eyes across a glass of champagne to his gaze

from the other side of the room   a room crowded with people

who had forgotten that every night was not like this one

gone for a decade   left just as winter turned to spring

each spring she takes hot tea to the porch in the morning

watches the patch of green between her and the river

waits for the heron to come   the great blue

he arrives alone   walks carefully across the turf

as if tender shoots might disturb balance   prehistoric torso

spindly legs   too old   too delicate for earth walking

she waits in silence until   the spread of ancient wings

he glides easily along the shore   he was made to fly

Redwings

fluttering flapping, red and black
in faded grass of early spring
a mating dance in cold clear air
his approaches, her rebuffs
high flight against bright blue
she embodies pure allure
teases, taunts until
she gets what she must have
a nest and eggs to sit upon
desire faint in memory
seductive red, sleek black
her lover, quiet now on thin bare branch
wondering
what was in it for him

The Weight of It

I see her tossing a small melon into the air, not high
just high enough to get a good feel for the weight
of it when it lands back in the spread of her palm.
She is young, perhaps eighteen, standing in a chilled grocery aisle
but she could be in the warmth of a garden patch.
She tosses it two or three times, assessing its weight, its worthiness
before placing it in her cart. She is dark-skinned in a store
where mostly white hands reach and touch tentatively
as one does in a small waspish Ontario town.
She will have a good life, I think. She has been schooled
by someone who understands the wisdom of weight
what it means to be solid in the world.
When I ask for a melon in the market in my Mexican town
the vendor inquires as to when I will eat it, selects one
and lifts it in both hands like the eucharist
draws it near to his face and, with eyes closed, inhales its aroma.
And like the young woman, melon rested firmly in her palm
his hands rub the rough skin, handle the heft of it,
know the worth of its weight.

Birds During a Pandemic

I have watched them closely and am drawn to their stories.

I stand at the screened door and watch an oriole attack a crow. Constant orange.
Steadfast black. The oriole flies to a high wire. The crow struts along the street —
try that again. When he lifts into flight, the orange dart makes a second strike.
Two more crows fly in as cover. The oriole retreats to a rooftop.
One crow follows and relaxes in beside him —
I'm not going to hurt you cousin, just a warning. You're no match.
The three crows gather for flight.
The tiny orange missile streaks in once more but alas, cannot control the battle
or inflict deadly damage.   The eggs are gone.
He must face his mate, small heart scorched and wounded like his sorrowed breast.

Through the Glass

There is a time of year when the lake goes green, the opaque green of pale jade. In late afternoon the sun washes the green wind-blown surface with a layer of pearl. These are the dog days, the days you forget until summer slows and you recall again that it will end. The great lake is finally warm enough for swimming. Soon pickerel will run beneath the moon, old loves will occupy the mind, and for a brief time you will forget that there is any other kind of day but this one. I thought I saw you again today, the clothes, the gait, the person you were. I strained to see through the glass but light bounced off the lake and I was pushed on by traffic. I adjusted the rearview mirror, tried once more for a glimpse of you.

Saturday Afternoon Confession

There had been a chill in the house for days, I don't remember why. Some disappointment, I suppose, some bitter unhappiness. We were small kids. Her silence was our suffering. I remember the Saturday afternoon. I saw her come out of the house into the brilliant sun, dressed up. I felt proud of her when she dressed up. She had a kind of look about her that I admired. Still, she did not speak, to Dad or to us, her children. She got into the car and drove off. She came back a different person, a different wife, a different mother. She spoke, she smiled — it was unfair, of course — her expectation of our gratitude, our compliance. We were compliant with relief. We were kids. Nothing was spoken.
We went back to our small lives, and were grateful. Dad did not comment ... it was about confession. She had gone off to Saturday afternoon confession. She had knelt in the wooden box and told the priest her troubles, confessed her sins against her family.
That meant she did not have to apologise or explain. She was forgiven. And now we were all to be released, to be thankful. That's what a Saturday afternoon confession did for a distressed family, made it possible for us to face each other again across an evening meal.

.

Los Más Bonitos

Are you leaving tonight?
Can you tell me the hour?
I saw you this morning in full flight, bodies tinged
pink by a sun not yet over the treeline
wing tip to wing tip in great geese formation
practicing, practicing…
Then tonight a low pass over the attic room
honking and barking your way into dreams.
Teach me the language of leaving
navigation by stars, night skyways to
the green agave.

I will know I am there when I walk home holding
a clear plastic bag of eggs, top twisted and tied in small knot.
The shells will be spotted brown, yolks rich, almost orange.
They will be from proud hens who rule the vendor's courtyard,
scratch around the pomegranate tree. She will hardly notice as
they enter and inspect her kitchen while she prepares at dawn.
Fresh eggs will be offered in wooden trays at her market stall.
Ocho huevos, por favor.
She will nod toward the farthest tray, instruct her daughter
to give me *los más bonitos*.

Los Antepasados

Mexicans are famous for the close unembarrassed connection they maintain with their dead, for home altars laden with food and drink for the ancestors as they return for *Día de los Muertos*, for the *tapetes* spread out for rest after the journey home, for *jarras* of cool water set out for refreshing before the celebrations.

I was a small child running my finger over names carved in black marble. My father took me to this place on summer Sundays after Mass, after he went to his garden, cut an armful of gladioli and placed them in a pail for me to hang on to as we drove to the cemetery. I knew his parents only from black and white photographs. They looked very old. In truth, they died quite young.

My father trimmed the gravesite while I carried the faded flowers to a heap of them at the back of the cemetery, stench of rotting foliage and foul green water smothering my senses. But the cemetery was large, and green, and treed. It did not frighten me. I knew it only in the bright light of summer, in the company of my Dad.

I like Mexican cemeteries best after the dead have left on the third day at the tolling of church bells. Flat tombstones covered with spent red and yellow flowers, gutted candles, scraps of food left over from meals taken at gravesides — all testimony to the affection families feel for *los antepasados*.

My father was a quiet man. He left quietly and did not, as far as I know, visit again. My mother, who always had to be heard, did come back, once, during *Samana Santa*.

Samana Santa

I was the only person in the street
on that quiet Good Friday
until you came
suddenly
with your old rush of energy
your tough spirit

my step slowed
my throat tightened
you left me with less breath

I stopped
started again
then turned toward home

you chose well
a quiet time
in a town that is seldom quiet

but I could not make you stay

I tried for a block or two
before giving in
before letting you fade

Mexico
of course it had to be Mexico
you knew you'd find me there

Evening Shades

It's late on a Saturday, a dry breeze brushing
blooms in the churchyard of San Martín,
old stone church as humble as the saint himself.
A funeral Mass and a handful of mourners to mark
the end of a life, ash in a box on the altar.
The pale priest elevates a chalice of wine
— *this is my blood* —
but the bloodied Cristo on the sidewall seems
disinterested, and the priest cannot remember
the name of the deceased, remembers only
to chide the gathered few
— *you too will one day be dust* —
My thoughts are of you and our northern river,
that place between islands, your ashes drifting
through liquid layers lit by sun, the dust
on my fingers touching my tongue
— *this is my body* —
Evening purples the worn hills of the Sierra.
Do the dead linger in this high dry desert,
in the ancient river?

The Bend in the Road

There's a great bend in the road that leads to San Marcos Tlapazola. From the vantage point of the vulture, high up in the thermals, the road is a white line tracking through fields of green agave toward a lone acacia tree. At the tree the road takes a turn west toward the foothills of the Sierra Madre and the distant pueblo. She always slows at the bend to have full view of the tree before rounding the curve. *That is where I want my ashes spread.* Friends take note and nod. *That is the spot*, and they drive on to the rugged little town and buy red pottery from the women there.

***

She walks through the field of green agave, small clouds of red dust trailing her, and places a weary hand on the trunk of the old acacia. The road has been widened and so the tree is now closer to the great bend, and with further widening, there may not be a tree. But it is here now and will be when they come with the ashes. She wants to feel steady with that thought. She watches the vulture circle against the intense blue of the sky, then looks across the gentle slope of the valley with its *milpas*, toward Oaxaca, tries hard not to forget the old city. She lived in Mexico for many winters, happy to abandon ice and snow, forever. She was never at home in the northern cold, even as a child. But neither did she harbour illusions of being at home in Mexico. She knew she was an outsider, a *güerita*. This does not lessen her attachment to the place or to her fading desire to linger near the tree. How much time in this dry breeze and shade? How long to register the pueblo in the foothills or the shadow of the vulture crossing the *milpa*? How long to recall that small serious child who was so suddenly old?

Swimming Lesson

As you eased your hands away
from my small body
you eased my fear,
bid me move differently in the world.
You were my big sister.
You taught me how to swim —
a stroke I have never forgotten.

I told you that story the year of your death.
You didn't recall the details,
seemed surprised by my gratitude.

You came to me in a dream last night
your voice through my phone.
I was in a dark place and fumbled
the phone, as one does in a dream.
I could hear you
and needed you
to hear me.
I groped for the phone in the dark
then woke.

Casa Divina

Small hotel on a rundown street, far from the best part
of town, attired in peptobismol pink like a
young woman the morning after a bad date, like an
old woman who still likes to dress up but can't quite
pull it off. There is something about you I admire, Divina,
distinguished among the well-worn of your street
dawn rays dappling through *banderitas* strung high
for a feast. What passes beyond flaking walls, Divina?
Lives gladdened and tarnished — *La Llorona,* old cantina
in the back, the weeping woman. The ordinary.
I will come to visit at night, *Divina*, when candlelight covers
your scars, when music and soft air and scent of spring
blossoms repair battered hearts, when patrons toast lovers
and their lovers past.

Gallina

His fondness for the *gallina* reflects in his dark eyes.
He is the creator, the sculptor who cast her in clay
in colours of the Mixteca, her ample hen body awash
in ochre and orange, umber and earth. She is flat bottomed
and hollowed out, a receptacle for eggs from his own small flock
which owns the patio outside the kitchen of the adobe structure
on the edge of the pueblo. There are many such pieces
around his place but seeing that my eye is taken
by this proud bird he quotes a price and slowly removes
the eggs from his prized *gallina*.
Now her noble presence rules my kitchen — handsome comb,
proud wattle, framing her beak — a reminder to don my N95
each time I leave the casa. I watch two women in the street
one masked in orange, one in brown. When saying adios
orange extends a hand, takes the brown beak between finger
and thumb, moves it up and down a little — stay safe.
Brown reciprocates, the same gesture — *cúidate amiga*
and then they part, bravely go their separate ways
into another day of contagion.

Like a Blue Sterile Cloth

Living in a country where one is not totally fluent in the language has its advantages, especially in Mexico where the background chatter is generally friendly and although you might understand a little, it plays like distant music, and this barrier of ignorance is like the privacy provided by the thin blue sterile cloth that the surgeon places over my face as I lie on a stretcher in her clinic. My head is to the side and there is an opening in the cloth exposing my ear where she will remove sun-damaged cells. When she speaks to me on the topic of my ear, I understand. I speak some Spanish. She speaks some English. Her name is Rosalita. Like many of her patients, I call her Doctora Rosi. She calls me Mrs. Lynda. We get by. When she gets down to the surgery she and her assistant chat quietly to each other about domestic matters. I understand little of their local jargon and assume she does this to fill the silence and create a normal atmosphere for the patient whose ear she is carving. Occasionally she asks through the blue cloth, *Are you OK Mrs. Lynda? Todo bien* I reply and am glad for the cool blue cloth. I can smile at her kindness, wince as she scrapes my ear. The cloth creates a safe space like that place on the edge or the outside where I am most comfortable. The Doc is very good at what she does. She writes a prescription for an antibiotic and a painkiller, and on my walk home I stop at a pharmacy and line up with others, ear bandaged and slightly throbbing. When it is my turn at the counter the young druggist looks at my prescription and then at me. I know that look — not unfriendly — merely, oh no, now I have to deal with a *gringa*. I speak to him in my textbook Spanish and he crinkles his brow and nods. He disappears into the back room to find the drugs. When he is totalling the bill he attempts some English. I don't understand. He points to a number on the box. *Oh*, I say, *the expiration date.* His shoulders droop. He looks at his shoes. *I try and I try*, he manages in stilted English. We smile and for a moment completely understand each other. He hands me the package.
Muchas gracias, I say. *Buen Día.*
Goodbye, he says. *Have a nice day.*

Pata de Elefante

You want to live in an old yellow house with a big iron gate, and behind it, a *Pata de Elefante*. During each winter spent in Mexico there comes a time when life slows to the pace at which it should be lived, when ease alters gait and senses adjust and accept the old city with forgotten affection. It is then that thoughts drift toward making this place home. There is a *casa* on Benito Juárez, yellow adobe with an ancient gate on the street. Just inside, a tall *Pata de Elefante*, long thin leaves draping its slim upper trunk like a woman's hair after her bath, falling on weathered shoulders. Seduction sets in: the aged gate, the gentle tree, the lemon-custard shade of adobe. A heavy door is recessed under an arch and a windowless facade leaves you free to consider a quiet inner courtyard, and from there shaded doorways to cool interior rooms. A worn wooden table reflects sunlight dappled by palms and a stone fountain spills its story. Great clay pots hug sun-soaked succulents, bright bougainvillea collude with warm walls. You want to turn a big iron key in a gate that knows you, rest a hand on the smooth trunk of an *Elefante*, pass through a familiar doorway, live in an old yellow house on Benito Juárez.

The *Pata de Elefante* is a tree endemic to Mexico. Its narrow trunk can grow to nine meters; its expanded base, which holds water, is often compared to an elephant's foot. Its foliage consists of long thin leaves said to resemble a fountain or a cascade of hair.

Someone Would Find It ...

At the clubhouse she noticed that the sweater was missing. She reported it and was sure someone would find it on a fairway, or beside a green, and turn it in. Golf was a relief. There had been a Great Blue Heron at the edge of the marsh on the 4th, tall on spindle-thin legs, still as a sphinx, blade bill ready for prey. She was aware that certain people raised an eyebrow about golf. But then, they were not poets. They had no instinct for stroke and arc, rhythm and pitch. The giant snapping turtle moved again across the grass with the weight of decades, the ache of another season without hatchlings. She had laid her eggs in a bunker, easy target for racoons. Someone would find it, turn it in. It was late in the season and a weekday, almost no one on the course. The sweater had been his, navy cotton with a crew neck. No matter that it was way too large. No matter. The unexpected warmth had brought her out, that and the autumn colours. Somewhere along the way she stuffed the sweater into the side pocket of her bag. Someone would turn it in. There had been a deer on the 7th, still as the heron until, ears flicked and she leapt over brush and into the woods for protection, for preservation. Someone would find it, turn it in.

All the Summer Birds Have Left

gone bright hits of colour
gone the chat of wrens, constant
call of cardinal, soft sounds
of doves in love

a new version of the same
dream last night, this time
lost in a labyrinth of blue
each door the wrong door

and your sister left outside
while you turned back, she
in the rain, you searching for
what you could not find

one old robin limps round
the garden, has she forgotten how
to fly or is she just too old
did her family leave without her…

there was a hard frost last night

What to Dream of Then

cicada songs ride warm breezes
through open windows
and I sleep, content that
summer lingers — still —

dark dreams bring dry leaves
blowing in the road
I heard them today
through the screen door
 — so what of tomorrow —

what if crickets forsake their song
and treefrogs go silent
if orioles leave in the night
and wedges of geese veer south

Ask Me Now

if you asked me now I'd say she tried to understand

there was a day when she tried to heal a small girl's loss
and the small girl was ungrateful
it was only about a turtle
a tiny shell found in mud at the edge of the pond
and then lost

I don't recall how she knew
if I told her   looked at her   wept
but later that day she stood above me   small brown bag in hand
I knew there was a turtle in it   and I knew I didn't want it
a store bought turtle wouldn't do

she took a shallow bowl from the top shelf
helped me with stones   water   store-bought turtle food

I was glad the day he left
managed the curved edge of the smooth bowl and lumbered away
across the grass
he was too big   too civilized   no match for the tiny shell in mud
at the edge of the pond

if you asked me now I'd say I should have tried to love him

On the last day of the world

the old woman slept in —
she loved dawn light and never slept late
but that day she missed it —
there were tasks to attend to
refresh the water in the birdbath
fill the oriole feeder
feed a friend lunch and after
walk in the garden, past its peak now
she loved it best like this...

the old woman read in her hammock in the screened porch
while waiting for four o'clock light, her favourite

Emily had a conservatory. Her father had it built against an exterior brick wall. Carpenters and masons created the glass space, just 6 by 17 feet, over two large dining room windows. In winter, heat from the Franklin stove passed through the open windows and kept the plants alive. The entrance was from her father's study. Emily called it her 'garden off the dining room'.

but she dozed off, and the book fell open
on the porch floor

Painkiller

fill my cup again

won't you

and fall with me

through stardust

making love along the way

like drunken angels

trying to recall bliss

let's pretend again

we know the way

our hearts repaired

with gin and olives

and tumble together

through starlight

and stop only

to dance the slow ones

Grateful acknowledgements to the editors of the publications where the following appeared.

Visitation, *Filling Station*, 2000

Ask Me Now, *Freefall*, 2000

Through the Glass, *Guernica Editions*, 2022

The Bend in the Road, *Guernica Editions*, 2022

Taking the Measure, *Guernica Editions*, 2022

I thought I saw us today, *El Portal* (Eastern University of New Mexico), 2023

The Weight of Two Oranges, *San Antonio Review*, 2023

On the last day of the world, *Dash Literary Journal* (CSUF), 2023

Saturday Afternoon Confession, *San Antonio Review,* 2024

All the Summer Birds Have Left, *Ink of Genesis Literary Journal*, (TL Publishing Group), 2024

You deserve a lover who takes away the lies and brings ... poetry.

Frida Kahlo

Lynda Wilde is a Canadian writer/photographer who lives between the cities of Kingston, Ontario, Canada, and Oaxaca de Juárez, Mexico. She is as attached to the semi-arid high desert of the Oaxaca Valley as she is to the rocks, trees, and lakes of Eastern Ontario. Her work has been published in literary journals in Canada and in the U.S.A.

Wintergreen Studios Press is an independent literary press. It is affiliated with the not-for-profit educational retreat centre, Wintergreen Studios, and supports the work of Wintergreen Studios by publishing works related to education, the arts, and the environment.

www.wintergreenstudios.com

www.ingramcontent.com/pod-product-compliance
Lightning Source LLC
Chambersburg PA
CBHW021000090426
42736CB00010B/1404